T0197094

The Story

of Our Lives

Jerry Schliep

authorHOUSE®

AuthorHouse™
1663 Liberty Drive
Bloomington, IN 47403
www.authorhouse.com
Phone: 1 (800) 839-8640

Published by AuthorHouse 02/27/2018

ISBN: 978-1-5462-2749-6 (sc)
ISBN: 978-1-5462-2748-9 (e)

Library of Congress Control Number: 2018901497

Print information available on the last page.

Contents

Dedication

This book is dedicated to Barbara, the love of my life!

Forward

This book is not required reading.

Introduction

"The best thing about the future is that it only comes one day at a time"
Abraham Lincoln

I am writing some of this book while having breakfast at SOB (South of the Border Cafe) up north in Grand Marais; it's a perfect place for my schedule because they open at 5 AM. Early to bed, early to rise! I believe that I might have a connection with Abraham Lincoln being that I was born on his birthday! It's probably a stretch; however, I tend to joke the way he did, between events or at different times. He would stop and tell a joke even in times of duress. I will think of different qualities like his along the way as I write this book. One that comes to mind, is Lincoln's concern for equality of life as his freeing of the slaves! Also, his belief in all human beings being very special with a brain to think!

CHAPTER ONE

Early Years

I found out a few things about the Schliep name. As a German name it signifies "a grinder of knives, scissors and the like." Schliep - to grind or sharpen. I am a true German. We have a Cookoo clock from Germany that I like. We bought it in Munich at a department store near the Glockenspiel. And I love German food like schnitzel.

My father's name was Arthur F. Schliep. He lived from 1908-1986. His dad was Reinhold and he lived from 1878-1957. His mother was Mary, she lived from 1890-1963. Reinhold came to the U.S. from Germany with his two brothers Gustav and August. I remember when August was living in Chicago. My mother, Lavern M. Schliep, lived from 1909-2001. Her maiden name was Emley. Christine Emley (her mother) lived from 1882-1966. Her father, William Emily lived 1883-1949. She had two sisters, Lola and Ina. In later years my mother sent Christmas cards that she made out of birch bark. She decorated each card individually with felt and ink; they were special. My grandmother Christine talked about riding to town on a cart pulled by oxen. She owned the American Bar and Hotel in Ladysmith WI. My grandfather was a barn builder and had some mental illness later in life. He was put in an insane asylum.

I was born on February 12, 1937 in Ladysmith, Wisconsin. My parents, Art and Lavern, were dairy farmers. I vividly remember in the early evening one day when I was about 7 years old, the sky was very dark and it sounded like a freight train was going to run over you. My father grabbed me around the waist and took me down to the basement. I remember this like it was yesterday! The tornado ripped off our open porch and lopped off the chimney. It also moved our machine shed to the Flambeau River; machine sheds had a dirt floor so it wasn't attached to the ground. It was lifted like a kite with the strong wind. Our huge barn was moved about six inches. We all survived without injury.

I went for a portion of my grade school in Ladysmith at our Lady of Sorrows Catholic School. I remember how a teacher, a nun, would hit your knuckles with a ruler if you were bad. I got rapped on the knuckles many times. At recess we played with marbles in the school yard. I cannot remember how the game was played - I think somehow your marble struck another and you claimed that one.

In 1945, our family – Jimmy, Herman, Donny, and I (I am the second oldest) - moved from Ladysmith to northern Minnesota upon recommendations by medical doctors because my mother and older brother Jim had asthma triggered by farm dust. My older brother missed one year of school because of the asthma.

Clearwater Lodge

It is located thirty miles up the Gunflint Trail out of Grand Marais, MN. It is still there and on the National Register of Historic Places. My father bought it with a partner in 1946. I lined the walls of a space near the front entrance of Clearwater Lodge with cedar and sold Minnesota moccasins, miniature birchbark canoes, miniature animals, T-shirts, etc. I really enjoyed selling so that was probably the start of my merchant days.

The lodge was built just after the CCC (Civilian Conservation Core) completed their work in the area creating portages, etc. The people who worked in the CCC stayed on to build the lodge. It was crafted with diamond willow furniture, dining tables with tree trunks as the base, chairs made with spruce logs with bark on and thick pine seats. The walls were formed with hewn logs. A huge stone fireplace was at the end. The walls were lined with mounted deer and moose heads plus hides of fur. There was a mail box built for the neighboring folks: on top was a mounted golden eagle.

Our mother worked hard at the resort cooking meals for the guests. At Clearwater we had housekeeping cabins (about 12 of them) and American plan with meals. She also kept the books, washed sheets, cleaned cabins etc. We hired girls to waitress and clean cabins. I started guiding guests when I was 12 years old – a fee of $12 per day plus tips.

At the reservation counter in an area next to the front entrance was a glass case where we sold candy bars. In an ice box behind the counter was pop including strawberry flavor and Fitger's beer. This room was lined with cedar bark with a birch bark ceiling.

The kitchen was a meeting place for guests. It had a big wood counter and cook stove plus a huge kitchen table and ice box. There was an old phone hanging on the wall for nearby resorts communication. There were different rings for each resort, it might ring once, twice, three times, etc. It was a party line.

The upstairs of the lodge had thirteen guest rooms lined with peeled spruce logs cut in half and positioned vertically. Each one of us boys had a room. My parents slept in a bedroom downstairs,

We had eight log cabins. All the cabins had wood heating stoves, ice boxes, and LP gas stoves for cooking. We delivered the ice and collected garbage once a week. The ice was stored in the ice house lined with sawdust. We would wash the sawdust off and, with ice picks and ice tongs, fill all the ice boxes, including the big one in the lodge kitchen. The garbage was hauled to the garbage dump. We had black bears come to the dump quite a bit. I had to kill a bear one night, shining it with a flashlight, because it was too aggressive and coming too close to the cabins.

Our winter school residence at Maple Hill near Grand Marais.
We are left to right: Jim, Jerry, Herman and Donald.

We put up ice each winter by clearing off a space on the lake; we skated on the space too. We would saw the ice to near the bottom of the frozen ice in squares lined up crisscrossed. Then, chop one ice block out of the lake and break the others off one by one; and float them down to the waiting truck. They were then slid up a ramp to the back of the truck and were driven off to the ice house truckload by truckload. It was packed in sawdust and it was amazing how the ice kept all summer.

I guided on Mountain Lake, a border lake with Canada because it was a favorite, very productive, trout lake. We would take a boat down Clearwater Lake about 5 miles with a 5 ½ horse Johnson outboard. I would carry the motor over the 88 rod (a rod is 16 ½ feet) portage up and down terrain.

I would carry the motor on my shoulders with a pad – the motor weighed about 35 pounds and of course I had to carry gas too. Sometimes on the guiding trips I would cook a shore lunch of fish for the guests and at other times my mother would pack sandwiches.

At Mountain Lake, we would troll with spinners and minnows. In spring and summer I guided near 30 days a month. We had about 20 boats on Mountain. We also had boats on Caribou, Deer Yard, Watap, and West Pike lakes. Each spring, it was our task to go to each lake to paint the boats, then put them in the water to expand the wood strips so they would not leak. I think all in all we had about 50 boats.

I fished for Lake Trout in the fall when they were spawning. The season closes the last day of September when they are up on particular gravel reefs. We would cast with Mepps spinners on the reef. You looked for a gravel area that was smoothed by the male trout. My favorite lake is Mountain, a border lake, and I know three reefs where they spawn. Also, I know of two reefs where they spawn on Clearwater Lake.

The rest of my grade schooling was at Clearwater School up the Gunflint Trail thirty miles from Grand Marais, Minnesota. The school was built by the local resort owners because the distance to Grand Marais was too far to travel twice a day. The school had grades one through eight; some grades had two students, or one, some none. There were 12 students in all. Our teacher lived at a resort across the lake from our resort. We knew when school was going to start when we could see her coming on snowshoes, about a mile away. While living at the resort in the winter, I did some trapping for weasel and mink. My youngest brother Don trapped beaver under the ice.

Our summers were sort of a Mark Twain thing. We built log rafts to go out on the lake. We stayed at Hedstrom's logging camp near Sucker Lake one summer, while my father was considering selling his interest in Clearwater Lodge to his original partner. I do not think partnerships in smaller businesses generally work out well. Also we spent another summer at Flour Lake Campground. We had a small trailer house plus a tent with a board flooring. There was a nice swimming beach.

High School

I went to high school in Grand Marais and graduated in 1954. During our high school years, in winter, my three brothers and I plus my mother some of the time would rent a house in Grand Marais so we didn't have to drive so far. In high school I could not play in sports because I had a hernia that was not operated on until my senior year. However, that gave me the opportunity to downhill ski. There was a ski hill operated with a rope tow on the bottom part of Sawtooth Mountain above Grand Marais. I skied there at night and weekends. I liked that it was a popular family sport and it was outdoors. I loved being outdoors.

In my senior year in high school, we went on our class trip to Southern Minnesota and Owatonna. We got back to Grand Marais late in the evening and I took Joan Bocovich and David Shold home and then drove home to Clearwater Lodge. I fell asleep about 12 miles up the Gunflint Trail and hit a pine tree. I was knocked unconscious. Some fishermen came by and had to take a crow bar to get a door open to get me out of the car. An ambulance took me to St. Mary's hospital in Duluth; the ambulance first topped at Dr. Smith's office in Grand Marais. I was unconscious. I woke up a little as we went through Two Harbors. I had a broken jaw and about 70 stitches. The horn rim in the older cars (it was a 1947 Plymouth) broke and cut my throat some; also I had stitches in my knee and arm. The car hit the tree squarely between the headlights with the steering wheel and the dash wrapped around me. I was very, very lucky!

In high school during summer, I continued guiding, this time on West Pike Lake that is about a mile portage from the east end of Clearwater. The lake trout go down deeper because cooler water at the surface warms up in July and August. The fish are down to about 60 feet. We would fish with steel lines, so when we trolled, the line would just stay down at a certain level depending how much line you let out. We used handmade fishing outfits, with a large reel and very stiff home-made rods; we put a small spring from a screen door at the tip of the rod so the steel line made a gradual bend. When we fished, we would work the pole back and forth to enhance the action of the lure. The lures were spoons such as a Doctor Spoon and a KB Spoon. The lake trout we caught in West Pike Lake were fairly large, from 3 to 10 pounds on average. It is a unique way of fishing when the trout are in deeper water. Usually, the lake was not crowded; most often we were the only boat on the lake. My father had only one boat stationed there.

My friend Bill from Forest Lodge and I took a few days trip up and down Arrow Lake that is adjacent to Rose Lake and all in Canada. It is 22 miles long. We set up a hand arranged sail in the canoe and with the westerly prevailing wind, we sailed all the way down this straight lake (so named Arrow Lake). I cannot remember if the wind changed for our return trip. Arrow Lake is entered by a small stream from Rose Lake. I remember a huge sandbar at the east end of Arrow Lake; westerly prevailing winds over the many years apparently formed that. We started at West Bearskin Lake (on the map looks like the shape of a mounted bear skin), then portaged to Dungan Lake, then the 180 stairs steps to Rose Lake and on to Arrow. My friend was appointed to the Naval Academy, probably not because of this trip!

My College Years

I saved enough from guiding and along with my parent's contributions to attend St. Johns University at Collegeville. At St. John's, tuition and board & room were $1,000 a year. Father Schmidt, pastor of St Johns Church in Grand Marais was my influence on going to St Johns. By the way, the church in Grand Marais, St Johns church was a mission church of St Johns Abbey and that is how I ended up at SJU.

I went there late. The lake trout fishing season ended the last day of September and I was guiding until then. Going to college late was not a good idea. The beanie season for freshman was over - that was good. I got a ride down to SJU with a tourist. I was dropped off in front of the church at SJU and the president of the college met me. I roomed in St. Benedict Hall with a guy from Duluth, a German Exchange student and another student. I was lucky to meet Jim Schneider; a senior from Duluth because he was the ski coach and was looking for someone to take over the program. I was then ski coach and team member for three years at SJU. We had our own ski hill, called Mt. Carmel, on campus; it had a rope tow.

Ski racing photo.

Coach and Captain Jerry Schliep

Our ski team with four members entered the four events during meets: downhill, slalom, jumping and cross-country. I skied all of them but downhill and slalom were my best events. I won a lot of them. We would have dual meets at St. John's too. I skied most every day at Mt,

Carmel. A priest, Fr. Conrad, and our ski team plus ski club members would go out each fall to cut weeds and small brush getting the hill ready for winter.

I was invited from the Central Division to participate in tryouts for the Olympics. I didn't go because western skiers were dominant and I didn't have time or money.

One more note on people that had cabins on Clearwater Lake – the O'Links from St. Cloud. He owned Stearns Mfg. One of his products was life preservers. He and his family would have me over for dinner at their house when I was at St. John's.

Favorite Memories /Barb wrote these/

I had three close girlfriends whom I met my freshman year in Mary Hall Residence, Peggy, Dixie and Barb. One night, we tiptoed down to the refectory to sneak a few homemade cinnamon rolls the nuns had just baked—they were irresistible!

In the St Ben's college brochure, there was a description of the ski hill located on the St John's campus. After class one afternoon, Barb Elmquist and I went over to try it out. With no warming hut, we nearly frostbit our feet it was so cold. However, we had so much fun, we made it a regular excursion. Father Conrad would come out and give us advice on skiing and soon we both grew confident with our abilities on the slopes. The cold afternoons were well worth it, for I met my future husband, Jerry Schliep, there on the Johnny slope.

Being a part of the warm and caring community of the College of St. Benedict taught me at a young age that close relationships with family and friends are the most important asset in one's life.

CHAPTER TWO

Getting Married and starting a family

My favorite picture. We are so much in love and so young!

Moving to Rochester

The Schliep kids in 1968.
from left, Karen, Monica and Kristin.

Daughters on stairs.

This photo was taken on the stairs going up from the original space of 800 square feet. We expanded upstairs and then to across the hall to another space. Our next move was to the present 2nd street SW location.

We moved to Rochester in the fall of 1965 to open our business. A classmate, John Morley from Forest Lake owned a moving business and moved us to Rochester at no charge. We rented an apartment at Silver Acres. It was fine, three floors and a deck; basement, first floor and upstairs. It had two bedrooms. Our three daughters shared the one bedroom!

We bought our home on <u>1028 Sierra Lane NE, Rochester</u> three years after we arrived, It had a great lot with no water problems and was on the lower part of the street. It also had a beautiful view of the valley; I like that better than looking at the city. You can still see the lights of the city at night though. Also, there are great sunsets! Our house is on the higher crest of street, not on lower part. Outside, it is redwood (like cedar) that is wonderful wood that is not easy to rot. The house is Frank Lloyd Wright inspired with a large overhang and large windows. Built in 1965, we bought it in 1969 just after opening our business for four years. Barb found the house and our being new in business, we thought the bank might not loan up the money I walked into the banker's office and he said sure. Barb loved the large windows too! I love the large overhang covering the deck. I think it is the best house on Sierra Lane and has the features we really love. It also has nice bombproof room under the garage. We went there during tornado or storm warnings.

We entered the kitchen right from the garage at the same level, which is very convenient. There are timbers in the open ceiling in the living room and we had a walk-out basement that Barb always wanted. Don't forget the large oak trees in the backyard.

CHAPTER THREE

Starting the Business

Here is the list of where I worked:

Gunflint Trail – Clearwater Resort, guiding, souvenir shop, helped run the resort through high school and college. Skied at Lutsen plus the ski hill in Grand Marais, Sawtooth Mountain Ski Area.

College – St John's University, B.A. in Business Administration, Ski Club & Ski Team. Skied every day!

Univac - 2 ½ years. Laid off because Univac operated having government contracts so business went up and down. It was a blessing because it forced me to get back into retail and small business, the place where I really wanted to be.

Cedar Hills Golf and Ski, manager. PSIA-certified ski instructor and ran ski school. I also ran the rest of business: food, rentals, and golf fees. I had a greens keeper!

Tatra Ski Shop. A lease store at Donaldson's Southdale plus manager of NW Ski and Sports Show in the Minneapolis Auditorium. Owner of sports show Paul Geyer at one time sent me to Colorado to get ski businesses to exhibit at the show. I got the 6&40 Motel, Winter Park,

Vail, Aspen, Crested Butte, and many resorts at the ski areas, such as Beaver Creek, to come to this.

We came to Rochester to open a ski shop. I went to the Minneapolis Public Library to search for per capita incomes of areas in Minnesota including the Twin Cities and Rochester where there were no ski shops. A few areas in the Twin Cities showed, up and also Rochester.

We opened the store in Rochester in the fall of 1965. I had no doubt that is was going to be successful. It was 800 sq. ft. of space; we got a SBA Loan - we had $15,000 in capitalization from them and $6,000 from us. I was fortunate to be able to borrow funds from relatives for part of the $6,000. We took over an upstairs apartment and then the apartment across the hall upstairs as we expanded. A good friend Bernie Dryer did a lot of the expansion work! We started the Tyrol Ski School. Eventually, we sent eight buses to area ski hills on Saturdays and fewer buses on Sundays.

There is nothing like owning your own business. You are totally in charge, no one to report to. If you make a mistake you do not have to report to anyone. The freedom of owning your own business is great! To have your own business, you look for a void in the market place. It is a niche thing!

We used the Franklin Covey System for managing. What a system! I was introduced to it by Robb Welch who worked at Abbott Labs in Salt Lake City. He later came to Rochester and began working at the store. I love that system, it sort of runs my life. You ranked things that need to be done by order of importance A, B, C and a number of things to do after each one. A's most important, etc. Then if for example you don't finish C's you transfer to the next day! I would recommend the system to all! The idea, I think, was developed by Franklin Roosevelt for his making notes for the coming day!

I expanded Tyrol to Mason City, Iowa. It went OK, maybe it was about break even. I sold it to Wayne Blaisdel after a number of years. I also expanded to Des Moines, Iowa for one year; then another shop opened so I decided to close. It is common for businesses to expand when successful in its original location thinking they can duplicate it. Many times it's not profitable.

I bought some land west of Tyrol in Rochester with plans to build our own building; however, getting close to my retirement, I decided not to do it and sold the land.

Mt. Frontenac offered to go into partnership with me but in business, those generally do not work out.

I joined SCORE (Service Corps of Retired Executives) for a while - I never thought I would volunteer. It was to mentor new or existing businesses. I was elected to chair the Southeastern Minnesota Chapter.

During our 38 years operating Tyrol the profit was fine and taking on patio and deck furniture was a blessing. It really helped our summer business; it was niche business, a void that was not filled at that time.

I joined Toastmasters for a while as I was not a good public speaker. Also, in classes at school I was not good at raising my hand to speak. It was an amazing success to me, even though skilled members did not realize my improvement. I eventually got a certificate!

CHAPTER FOUR

My philosophy

On Virtues

According to Webster's Dictionary – "Moral excellence and righteous; Goodness." I used to think the only virtues were Faith, Hope and Charity. I was on a plane trip sitting next to women who said she was on her way to give a retreat on patience to nuns. She said that was a virtue as well as said there are so many virtues. A virtue is developed by practice!

My Philosophy

I have a lot of faith in God. He watches over me and plans ahead for me! It is fantastic! He is ahead of me with the proper steps for a good life.

"You give and you get."

"You are what you eat."

"God helps those who helps themselves."

Mentoring is good because all of the experience someone has can be transferred to another (at least part of it).

I like the Benedictine Values. The headings are as follows: Awareness of God, Moderation, Hospitality, Dignity of Work, Community Living, Listening, Taking Counsel, Common Good, Truthful Living, Stewardship, Respect for Persons, and Justice. I received a copy on the rules of St Benedict at an Alumni meeting program.

I like this by poet Robert Frost. "I took the less traveled road and that made all the difference."

Poems I wrote to Barb

Dearest Barb, the love of my life! I want to hold your hand! You hold my hand so tight with all your might. Our love has grown forever since we have been together. Love, Jerry!

Human life is such a treasure, you cannot measure. Every day is a gift from God, not to nod! God paved the way for Barb and I you cannot even imagine. We have a lot of faith and he leads the way! What more can I say!

Poem from Jerry – March 24, 2013

I love you Barb, with your disease; you are quite at ease!
That is a virtue at heart, we will never be apart!
God will guide us through, you and I!
You have the gratitude in your attitude, for the life we have had!
Compassion is our strength to give us life, for God has
a place for us!
I know, everlasting peace!
I love your smile!
I love you Barb!
Jerry

Another poem I wrote relating to mindfulness.

"Oh Quaking Aspen"

Oh Quaking Aspen, you are so relaxing!

The wind blows even without my asking.

The breeze makes me feel so much at ease.

You are so kind to please!

I think of this as mindfulness.

Thank you for your kindliness.

Oh Quaking Aspen, you are so relaxing!

CHAPTER FIVE

Health and Recreation

Through many dangers, tolls and snares, I have already come; tis grace hath brought me safe thus far, and grace will lead me home.

Barb's Illness

The Lewy Body Dementia disease she had was a fairly new type of dementia. I cannot remember a lot of changes in the progression. I know she could not pay the bills anymore. She would always give me a good night kiss! The Parkinson's portion of the disease progressively affected her walking. She had always been so active! I remember clearly when Jeanne, our live-in caregiver, would take her for a walk down the hall at our house. She would appear so contented as she was able to do it somewhat! Barb loved the water, she went with her girlfriends to the RAC pool for some time even when she had the dementia. I remember specifically our daughters helping her into the water off our dock at Pike Lake where we had our cabin - it was such a pleasure for her.

We had many times when in her wheelchair Jeanne taking her down the street. We all sat on our driveway many times in the sun - she in her wheelchair.

We were so lucky to have her, she did wonderful things. Every morning she would give Barb a shower and dress her in a wonderful way. She prepared all out meals and we had people come in from Home Instead to relieve her at times. Jeanne was with us though all of Barb's later years. We were able to do this because we had long-term care policy that included in-home care. We were one of the earliest policyholders; so it was a better policy as insurance companies got claim experience. For a number of years when Barb was in-home with her sickness of Lewy body we collect about $85,000 per year for caregiver expenses.

Barb loved the fall season-we were married in the fall of 1960-on October 15th. She would love the fall colorings of the leaves! Writing like this brings tears to my eyes.

Barb slept a lot during her disease. I would go in her room and sit for a time while she was sleeping.

Barbara passed away September 18, 2015 in our bedroom.

Mom and Jeanne.

"This is Jeanne, out fulltime caregiver."

I have obsessive compulsive disorder that showed up early in life when I would take a boat to a portage and I would obsess too much on whether it was tied up correctly. It was identified by an expert in my middle age.

There were some positives because it helped me focus on certain things; it can also control your life too much. Overall, I don't think it interfered too much with my life.

I talk about it more now that I am now not in business at the ski shop. It is something you tend to hide for some time. I went to five OCD National Conventions, three with Barb; Tennessee, Atlanta, Chicago, Minneapolis, Washington D.C. As I have said before, most people with the disease use self-therapy and some form of medication. Self-therapy includes ERP (enter response prevention) and CBT (cognitive behavior therapy). Both help! I am so happy that I found out what I had and what to do for it.

My new knees

What a gem! I am so lucky to live in an age when this is done! I had the first operation on May 15, 2017. I now have gained ten years of enjoying sports activity. Getting it done was a process, - two nights in the hospital for each knee. I remember one night getting out of bed and rolling on the floor. The nurses were so nice! At home recovering, our daughters helped so much! I remember calling Monica who was sleeping next door at our house to bring me coffee in bed! The opioids (oxycodone) worked so great to sleep and ease the pain. I never thought I would get off them, but through a lot of effort, it happened. Now I am mobile!

Walking with poles

I like to walk with poles called Nordic Walking. It gives your upper and lower body exercise plus cardio. I use Leiki hiking adjustable poles. They give you support for your knees and support for walking. I know where you can buy the poles -Tyrol Ski & Sports, Rochester.

Pike Lake

We spent many family vacations at Pike Lake. My parents owned the Pike Lake resort from 1960-1973. During one of our vacations, always looking for a cabin of our own, I saw one we liked. Upon arriving home, we found out it was going to be sold. We were so excited that Karen and I drove up the next day and bought it in 1984. The cabin was built in 1948 and has an ultimate location on the North Shore with a southern exposure. Barb was always big on locations on the north shore of lakes because of the southern exposure. An early resident of Pike Lake said that the first cabin built on the lake was at our location. Pointing out that it's the first cabin you see driving down Pike Lake Road and first see the lake. The location has nice high ground sloping downward on both sides. The ground is shale, drains real well, never standing water. Properties on both sides are lower. A note of interest, there is a strong spring running under the property. This area in front of the cabin stays open all winter. There was a hand pump by the lake to get spring water. Also, I heard owners of the cabin years ago had a wooden box by the shore of the lake where the spring runs in to cool milk, etc. (a rustic fridge). The pipe to the well still exists. I want to hook it up sometime with the hand pump that is in the shed and the long pipe under the cabin. They had a rowboat that they stored via rollers under the cabin (it was a wood strip boat). That type of boat sometimes would be put in the water to expand the wood strips so it would not leak! Pike Lake is very clear. With a Secchi disc you can see down 21 feet. Pike Lake is known to be the second clearest lake in Cook County after Clearwater Lake. We also have the west prevailing wind coming down the lake towards the cabin. Because of the wind, lakes in this area have sandy beaches on the east ends as Pike Lake does.

Steamboat Springs

We have been so lucky with our locations- home, cabin and condominium! The condo is in Storm Meadows East Slopeside. I think it's the best ski-out, ski-in in Steamboat! From the fourth floor you go down about 6 steps, past a one bedroom condo and ski right down to Right-a-Way run. And when coming home you ski right up to the condo! It has a good view of the slopes too. The entrance to the building is on the 6th floor.

We first got to Steamboat invited by Jack Perkins. He was a sales rep for ski equipment and clothing. He had a condo there. The Hart rep had a home in Steamboat as well. Both were instrumental in starting our store in Rochester.

Steamboat has the lightest powder anywhere called champagne power, as it comes across a desert from the west and is the driest. Most people would not know the difference from the rest of Colorado. Steamboat, best in the west and the World!

My Cars

I had two sports cars. I had a Ford Probe and a Ford Mustang- which I still have. Both were bought new, the Mustang is a year 2000 with currently about 65 thousand miles.

My first car was a 1950 Ford. As I recall, it was given to me by a guest at our resort. The woman and man had been friends and special guests for many years. O'Leary was their name! Other friends the McGill's had a cabin on Clearwater Lake. In the winter he was a Black Jack dealer in Las Vegas. They gave me a camera for my high school graduation present. Back to the cars. I loved that '50 Ford, gray in color, 2-door and had a rocket piece in the middle of the grill. Then my next car was a 1950 Studebaker (pea green), four-door with overdrive.

It had 2 quite large rocket projections, one on each side of the front of the car. The next car was a 1961 Ford, this one Barb and I were going to take to Chicago on our honeymoon. However, it was not in good shape so we took the train. Then I had a new Ford Falcon bought from a Ford dealer on Grand Avenue in St. Paul. Then more cars after that. I now have a 2005 Jeep wrangler that drives like a car but challenges tough roads.

The Outdoors

Grouse hunting is one of my favorite hobbies. Ruffed grouse seem to be on a ten-year cycle as far as population numbers. They are known to be the best eating upland game bird, by far. In the winter they dive from trees into the snow to keep warm. I have been snowshoeing and a grouse rose up out of the snow and alarmed me. When hunting them in the fall you can spot their shape from quite a distance. They survive in the winter by eating aspen buds, etc. They are a breeze to clean. I save only the breast. I have been hunting them since high school. I drive old roads early in the morning drinking my coffee. I walk to hunt them too- great exercise!

Fly fishing is a good activity, a dynamic sport with all the weight of rods, lines, size of flies, tippets, etc. It gets you out in the country by water too, which is relaxing. Catch-and-release is good, however if there are plenty of fish it's no problem taking some to eat. Also, trout are a good source of fish oil. I am a member of Trout Unlimited.

I had the opportunity to fish in Alaska (near Bristol Bay) a number of times with a friend from Steamboat Springs. We fished for Silver Salmon (known as Coho in Lake Superior) using stout fly rods on the Togiak River.

Skiing is the best family sport! Each person can ski where they like and with whom. The social aspect is wonderful, as well as having lunch in the chalet, the exercise you get, plus enjoying winter. I took a ski trip to Chile, South America a few years ago. I had always wanted to ski in the southern hemisphere during our summer months. I had been doing some research on where to go in Chile, and Valle Nevado was rated one of the best. I went with Tom Hall and his wife Leslie. We flew into Santiago Chile and took a shuttle up to the area, one hour away and with sixty switchbacks. There are three hotels at Valle Nevado. Our ski package included dining at each hotel. It was a great trip!

Another memorable ski trip was heli-skiing in Golden, British Columbia some years ago. Something I had also always wanted to do. The group included some doctors from the Mayo Clinic.

CHAPTER SIX

Humor

My father's jokes

He would be holding his head and was asked "what's the matter grandpa?" He would reply "I was putting toilet water on my hair and the seat fell down."

"I take a bath once a year whether I need it or not! I found two sets of underwear I never knew I had."

When fishermen came to the resort, the first thing they would do is go on the dock and say "how's the fishing?" and grandpa would say "it should be good because none have been caught for over a month."

He said Iowa fishermen would come to the resort and they would have a new pair of striped overalls and a five dollar bill. They would not change either the entire time.

Jerry's humor

When I leave a group, I say "I am leaving now, no tears please" Also another one, "You are not so bad either!"

I will ask "Are you in charge?" They most often say "In charge of nothing".

And then I might say, "I don't care about what your wife says about you, I think you're ok."

I am like Lincoln with telling jokes, he told them at unusual times, even in times of duress.

Over the years I seemed to develop extra names for employees such as "Mickey" for Mike Pattinson, "Angel" for Angela, "Vonski" for Von Sheridan.

A few Sven and Ole jokes

Sven vent to the eye doctor. The doctor says you got a cataract? Sven says, no, I have a Lincoln Towncar!

Ole says to the doctor at the Mayo Clinic, "I got a problem. I have a big bowel movement at six in da morning every day. Doctor says "that sounds perfectly normal, why are you so worried about it?" Ole: "yah, but I don't vake up till seven!"

Ole and Sven went fishing one day in a rented boat and were catching fish like crazy. Ole said "We better mark this spot so we can come back and catch more fish." Sven then proceeded to mark the bottom of the boat with a large 'X'. Ole asked him what he was doing, and Sven told him he was marking the spot so they could come back tomorrow to catch more fish. Ole said, "ya big dummy, how do ya know ve are going to get da same boat tomorrow?

Ole and Lena got married. On their honeymoon trip they were nearing Minneapolis when Ole put his hand on Lena's knee. Giggling, Lena said "Ole you can go farther if you vant to." So Ole drove to Duluth.

Ole died. So Lena went to the local paper to put in an obituary. The gentleman at the counter, after offering his condolences, asked Lena what she would like to say about Ole. Lena replied, "You yust put 'Ole died!'" The gentleman, somewhat perplexed, said, "That's it? Just 'Ole died?' Surely, there must be something more you'd like to say about Ole. If it's money you're concerned about, the first five words are free." So Lena pondered for a few minutes and finally said, "O.K. you put 'Ole died. Boat for sale.'"

Chapter Seven

Later life

In the years operating Tyrol, our personal lives were full and enjoyable. Barb played a lot of tennis which she was good at. She swam a lot at the Rochester Athletic Club (RAC) and had an active bridge group. Plus our time at our cabin up North and the condo in Steamboat!

I, of course, ski a lot, both downhill and cross-country. Downhill at Welch Village and Steamboat; cross-country up north and around Rochester. Previously I did some downhill ski racing at Welch Village with a group of guys, our team was called "Gate Thrashers". I attended downhill ski demo's in the Midwest but even more in Colorado

I do some fly fishing in southeastern Minnesota, primarily the Whitewater State Park area.

We were fortunate to take many trips to Florida, many of them with Stephanie's family. We would walk the beach every morning and the sound of the waves was mesmerizing. Each resort that we stayed at had a swimming pool and the water was one of Barb's favorite enjoyments.

My goal for the future is to do more woodworking, especially with diamond willow. There is quite a lot of it found in the low areas "up north". I already have made some lamps with spruce and aspen. I am making a coffee table with a toboggan turned upside down. It will have a diamond willow support and a glass top. Years ago I made a foot stool out of diamond willow. It is a sturdy wood and therefore you see a lot of walking sticks made out of it! I have other activities that I'd like to do more. These include cross country classic skiing and Nordic walking with poles. Snowshoeing with poles too. I would also like to start reading more.

I recently rejoined the Rotary Club of Rochester. I had been a member for 35 years, before taking a couple of years off. There are a lot of people I know there and will nurture my social agenda.

I sold our two-bedroom condo a year ago. The condo in Steamboat was purchased for pleasure, with the goal of breaking even each year. We have many good memories of trips there with family and friends. My plan when I bought "Cabin Sweet Cabin" was to rent it and fix the studio for rent. The rental income was to augment my Social Security. A lot of people have social security along with a pension from the company they worked at. When I look back I realize that we have spent a lot of money in ways which I do not regret. Both cabins are now renting quite readily, so hopefully they will help with the flow of money. And it's looking like my plan will work out as I imagined after all!

I am writing this book for my own purpose, the grandchildren and the encouragement of my daughters. I am renting my properties which include two cabins and one condo. I am in the process of downsizing not upsizing.

Here is what my kids and grandkids are doing now. Karen is a Professor of Public Health at the University of Utah. She lives in Salt Lake City with her husband Alan. Their daughter, Monica Ruth, is attending Northeastern University in Boston, MA. Monica has retired from being a classroom health teacher and is now certified to teach online. This has allowed her more freedom. She and her wife Carrie live in Minneapolis with their two dogs Dougie and Gracie. Kristin and her husband Robb took over the family business – Tyrol Ski & Sports with continued success. Kristin previously worked as a Physical Therapist. They have two kids. Aly is a senior and Eric a sophomore, both at Century High School. All my kids enjoy sports and outdoor recreation. Monica Ruth rows on the varsity Crew team in college. Alyson runs track, cross country and participates in Nordic ski racing. Eric runs track and cross county as well as skis on the Alpine ski team.

*"**We can complain because rose bushes have thorns, or rejoice because thorn bushes have roses.**"*
Abraham Lincoln.

Postscript

I want to sincerely thank all who participated in writing this book, my three daughters, Aunt Stephanie Helgesen and friend John Weiss.

Printed in the United States
By Bookmasters